Travel Games for Kids

Woo! Jr. Kids Activities Founder: Wendy Piersall

Book Layout and Cover Design by: Lilia Garvin
Production Designer: Ethan Piersall

Published by DragonFruit, an imprint of Mango Publishing, a division of Mango Publishing Group, Inc.

For permission requests, please contact the publisher at:

Mango Publishing Group
2850 Douglas Road, 4th Floor
Coral Gables, FL
33134 USA
info@mango.bz

For special orders, quantity sales, course adoptions and corporate sales, please email the publisher at sales@mango.bz. For trade and wholesale sales, please contact Ingram Publisher Services at customer.service@ingramcontent.com or +1.800.509.4887.

Travel Games for Kids

ISBN: (p) 978-1-68481-043-7
BISAC: JNF021040, JUVENILE NONFICTION / Games & Activities / Puzzles

How to:
License Plate Game

Put a check mark on each state's license plate that you see on your trips!

Keep in mind that each state can have multiple license plate designs, so keep your eyes out for ones that don't match the images provided!

ILLINOIS

☐ ALABAMA

☐ COLORADO

☐ ALASKA

☐ CONNECTICUT

☐ ARIZONA

☐ DELAWARE

☐ ARKANSAS

☐ FLORIDA

☐ CALIFORNIA

☐ GEORGIA

☐ HAWAII

HAWAII
MNG 728
ALOHA STATE

☐ KANSAS

KANSAS
123 SAM

☐ IDAHO

Scenic IDAHO
1A WJ785
FAMOUS POTATOES   02

☐ KENTUCKY

Kentucky
UNBRIDLED SPIRIT
333 XDB
CAMPBELL   02-18

☐ ILLINOIS

ILLINOIS   05-19
AU 73671
LAND OF LINCOLN

☐ LOUISIANA

Louisiana
TXK 512
Sportsman's Paradise   17

☐ INDIANA

INDIANA
999AAA

☐ MAINE

MAINE   APR
6992 LH
Vacationland   04

☐ IOWA

IOWA
ABC 123
AUG   COUNTY

☐ MARYLAND

Maryland
MD PROUD

☐ MASSACHUSETTS

JUL *Massachusetts* 12
10787
The Spirit of America

☐ MONTANA

TREASURE STATE 02 18
6·68450B
MONTANA - 10

☐ MICHIGAN

PURE MICHIGAN   SEP
DJV 1825
michigan.org

☐ NEBRASKA

· NEBRASKA · 8
VIB 529
1867   2017

☐ MINNESOTA

EXPLORE Minnesota.com
457·MKZ
SEP   10,000 lakes   14

☐ NEVADA

NEVADA
890·H14
· Home Means Nevada ·

☐ MISSISSIPPI

MISSISSIPPI
RAF 660
RANKIN   10-13

☐ NEW HAMPSHIRE

LIVE FREE OR DIE
305 4929
6   HAMPSHIRE   2012

☐ MISSOURI

AUG   MISSOURI
BICENTENNIAL
MO2 021
1821 ★ 2021

☐ NEW JERSEY

New Jersey
C90·ELE
Garden State

- [ ] NEW MEXICO
- [ ] OKLAHOMA
- [ ] NEW YORK
- [ ] OREGON
- [ ] NORTH CAROLINA
- [ ] PENNSYLVANIA
- [ ] NORTH DAKOTA
- [ ] RHODE ISLAND
- [ ] OHIO
- [ ] SOUTH CAROLINA

☐ SOUTH DAKOTA

☐ VIRGINIA

☐ TENNESSEE

☐ WASHINGTON

☐ TEXAS

☐ WEST VIRGINIA

☐ UTAH

☐ WISCONSIN

☐ VERMONT

☐ WYOMING

How to:
Funny Fill-in Stories

Fill in the stories with any word of the type asked for, such as verb, noun, adjective, etc., and then read your funny story.

Make sure to use a pencil if you're writing them, so you can erase and share the fun!

Traveling to the Big City

The _____ city is a _____ place to
    (adjective)   (adjective)

_____ to because there's so much to do!
(verb)

There are so many _____ buildings
                 (adjective)

and sights to _____ . You can _____ a
         (verb)   (verb)

_____ at the theater, where people
(noun)

_____ and _____ to _____
(verb)   (verb)   (adjective)

music. There are all kinds of museums

to visit, like the _____ _____
               (adjective)   (noun)

museum or the _____ _____
             (adjective)   (plural noun)

museum. I like going to the zoo

when I visit the city, where we can

see animals like _____,
           (plural noun; animals)

_____ or my favorite,
(plural noun; animals)

the _____ _____ .
    (adjective)   (plural noun; animals)

Let's go Camping

My family and I are going camping near a

_____ _____ this summer. Camping is
(adjective)   (noun)

_____ because you get to _____ and
(adjective)   (verb)

_____ outside. When we _____ to the
(verb)   (verb)

campground, we set up our _____ ,
                              (plural noun)

where we will _____ at night. We like to
                  (verb)

go _____ in the _____ , hoping to
    (verb -ing)   (noun)

_____ some _____ fish for dinner.
(verb)   (adjective)

We also go _____ in the _____
              (verb -ing)   (adjective)

_____ , hoping to spot wildlife like
(noun; place)

_____ or _____ . My
(plural noun; animals)   (plural noun; animals)

favorite part about camping is _____
                                    (verb -ing)

_____ over the campfire.
(plural noun; food)

RiDing the Ferry

A ferry is a type of _____ that is
(noun; vehicle)
_____ than a ship. Ferries let people
(adjective)
_____ _____ from town to _____
(adverb)   (verb)   (noun; place)
across the water. Some ferries let you _____
(verb)
your car in the _____ so you can _____
(noun)   (verb)
it on a nearby island. It costs _____
(noun; number)
dollars to _____ the ferry. Some ferry
(verb)
rides have _____ shops where you can
(adjective)
buy _____ for the ride, like _____
(plural noun)   (noun; food)
and _____. It's _____ to look for
(noun; food)   (adjective)
_____ and _____ _____
(plural noun; animals)   (adjective)   (plural noun; animals)
_____ in the water along the way.
(verb -ing)

A Family RoaDtrip

This summer my family is taking a _____
(adjective)

trip in our _____ . We are driving
(noun; vehicle)

_____ miles to visit our
(noun; number)

_____ in the state of _____ .
(plural noun; people)   (noun)

My parents _____ lots of snacks like
(verb)

_____ , _____ , and my
(noun; food)   (noun; food)

favorite, _____ _____ with _____
(adjective)   (noun; food)   (adjective)

_____ to drink. We also _____
(noun; beverage)   (verb)

games to play in the _____ , like
(noun; vehicle)

_____ the _____ and _____ like a
(verb)   (noun)   (verb)

_____ _____ . It's a _____ drive
(adjective)   (noun)   (adjective)

but we have fun _____ together on
(verb -ing)

vacation.

Taking the Train

I love _____ on a train from my
  (verb -ing)

_____ to the _____ city. Trains
  (noun; place)   (adjective)

are _____ because they _____ on
  (adjective)   (verb)

special _____ made of _____
  (plural noun)   (noun)

instead of roads. It's fun _____ for the
  (verb -ing)

train and _____ the _____ sound
  (verb -ing)   (plural noun)

as the train arrives. While _____ on the
  (verb -ing)

train, I like to look out the _____ and
  (plural noun)

see the countryside, passing _____,
  (plural noun; places)

_____ _____, and _____
(verb -ing) (plural noun)   (adjective)

_____ as we _____ past.
  (plural noun)   (verb)

We're Going on... an AirPlane!

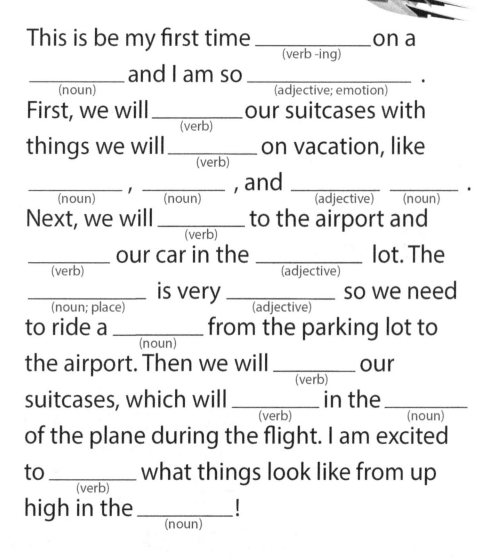

This is be my first time _____ on a
(verb -ing)

_____ and I am so _____ .
(noun)   (adjective; emotion)

First, we will _____ our suitcases with
(verb)

things we will _____ on vacation, like
(verb)

_____ , _____ , and _____ _____ .
(noun)   (noun)   (adjective) (noun)

Next, we will _____ to the airport and
(verb)

_____ our car in the _____ lot. The
(verb)   (adjective)

_____ is very _____ so we need
(noun; place)   (adjective)

to ride a _____ from the parking lot to
(noun)

the airport. Then we will _____ our
(verb)

suitcases, which will _____ in the _____
(verb)   (noun)

of the plane during the flight. I am excited

to _____ what things look like from up
(verb)

high in the _____ !
(noun)

What is the smallest bridge in the world?

The Bridge of your nose.

What goes uphill and downhill, and always stays in the same place?

A road.

How to: Mandala Mazes

The goal of these tough mandala mazes is to enter at the arrow pointing in, and exit at the arrow pointing out.

Why should a man always wear a watch when he travels in a desert?

Every watch has a spring.

Why will a traveler never starve in the desert?

Because of the sand which is (sandwiches!) there.

How to: Hangman

One player thinks of a word or phrase & the other player tries to guess it. Have them suggest a letter, but they can only make a certain amount of wrong guesses before the game ends. If they guess right, fill in all instances of that letter. They can also guess the final word(s). For every wrong guess, draw another part of the hangman.

Parts include:
Head, Body, Right Arm, Left Arm, Right Leg, and Left Leg.

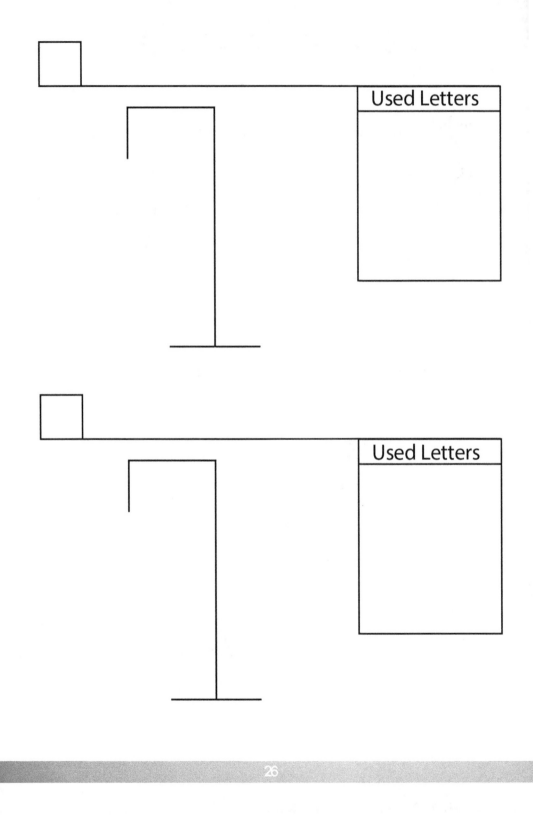

Used Letters

Used Letters

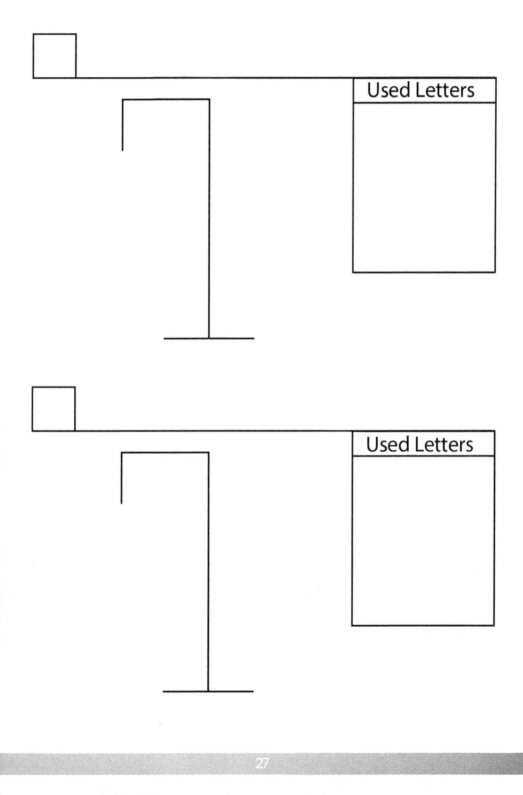

Used Letters

Used Letters

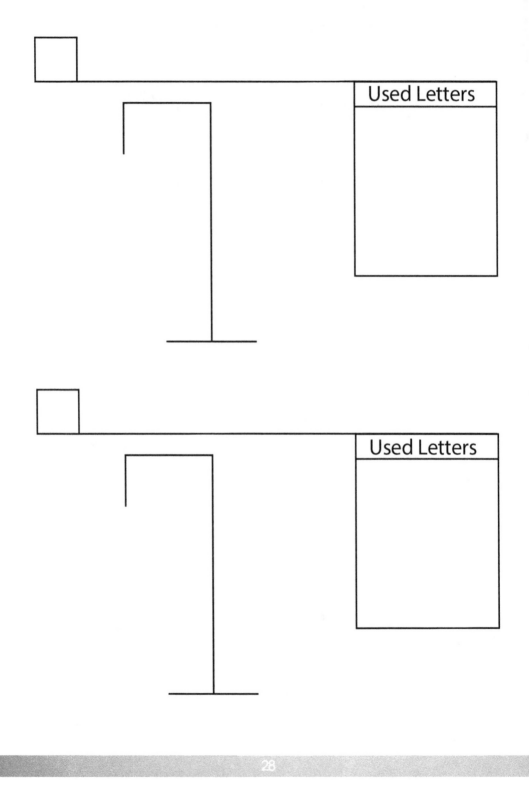

Used Letters

Used Letters

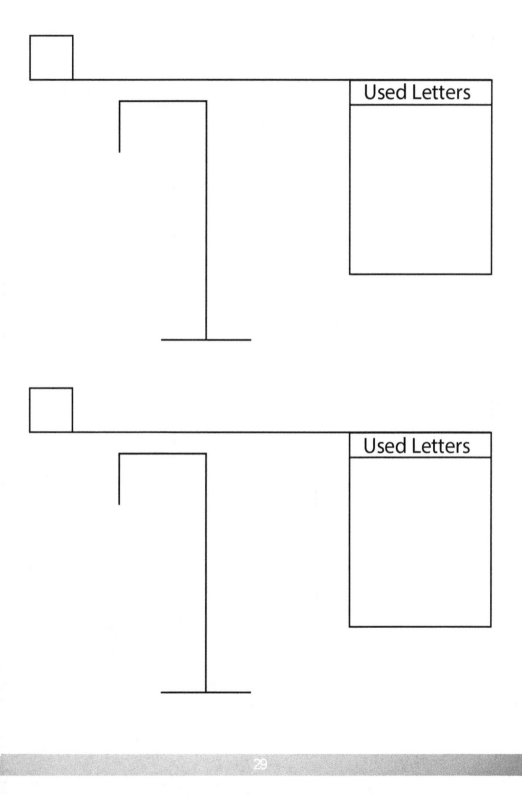

Used Letters

Used Letters

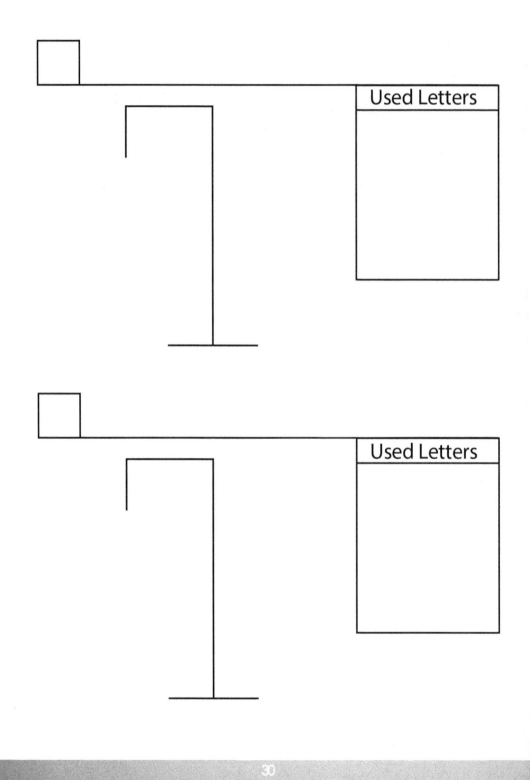

Used Letters

Used Letters

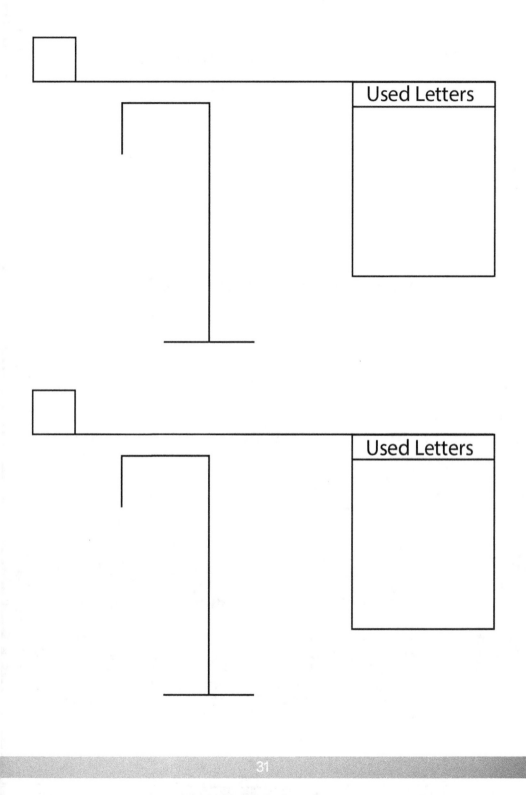

Used Letters

Used Letters

What has a face, but no head, hands, or feet, yet travels everywhere and is usually running?

A watch.

When must your shoes be left outside of your hotel?

when they won't go over the inn-step.

How to:
Word Search

Find the listed words inside each page's puzzle. Words can be hidden horizontally, vertically, diagonally, forward, and backward, so keep your eye out for them in each direction!

```
B E Z J R N E P O A C X D S
A S T V O F V S L J S I N N
Q E Y A S G H E L H R F R A
D C R E T Z D T R E H O U C
E Q M A U S Q O C T Y Y T K
K A R E T N Y T S U I Y U S
G G L Q H S I X Y X Q B S C
R R R E W O E B Z G U E L J
B T G H N A F R K O I V X E
G V Y S C O O L E R B Q L H
```

COUNTRIES WORD SEARCH

Australia
Bhutan
Brazil
Bulgaria
Canada
Chile
China
Ecuador
Egypt
England
Iceland
India
Iraq
Ireland
Japan
Mexico
New Zealand
Nigeria
Peru
Poland
Scotland
Senegal
Slovenia
Somalia
Spain
Switzerland
Ukraine
USA
Vietnam

```
X M C Z J V R N D P D S G L
V J A Q F X E G T N O J S B
E U U N C L Y P A M B P O N
M D B J T A H L A B H V N C
R E Z M N E R L T Q A R H I
I Z X V B E I F N W X I S C
I R H I Z A T V D Q L Z X I
A B A T C N G L N E S X T K
B U I Q J O I X A N E X A K
Y W S E Z Z S R L Z T R P I
S A U T A B X E G S A F E Z
S C M R R K G T N E T G R A
N R B Q F A Q K E N S C U E
T I J N H R L G E E D R T A
P T G I W G Z I C G E G D I
A I N E V O L S A A T O C D
L C E F R R D A D L I B N N
X F R Z J I J N G Q N U A I
N X W O S P A I N J U L T W
J H A I D L A M H A Q G U W
N E W Z E A L A N D S A H P
A Y Y C T S U A Y C P R B G
D Z I A R P P C O F O I Z U
C A N A D A Y T E K L A E Y
O H Z J J Y L G M R A K M A
X I R E L A N D E N N Y K O
I O V A N I H C U S D Q F C
J G A D E N I A R K U Y F N
S K O W Z Z Y N X A T J M A
```

GEOGRAPHICAL FEATURES WORD SEARCH

```
Y Q M K D G B X Y J M F H F
E Z W N E E D U U F I G O M
L U E O L N S O T X H R O M
L Z Z X U A S E M T E H A O
A G E O R Z J G R S E P X Q
V N S Y W E Y T T T J Z X O
Z M I V L R O C C Q Y C N R
U U P E N I N S U L A A A E
R Z D N A L S I P V C V U V
B A S I N L K W O L L N W I
X Q I S L N B M O S B Q B R
I E K O U M A V D U U D U C
R B T N N M V E R N Y I I D
T A R E V K H D C D T V E H
R E I C A L G T E O Y I F G
T L U A F O C L S T J D L M
T H M H R C T A T I U E U M
M X I S V A P F V D A W Y O
I W X G T K C R S E E D K U
C D N W H T E E T P T R K N
A Y N R J L A U I E A J S T
M K V A P M A A E P L X Z A
C A N Y O N M N T R P Q E I
I V W U L X E A D I M A C N
D T N A N B Y X E P Q A R H
Q T K U F F L L C R A X E I
T E N Z M Y G F T G T C E L
N P X B H T H J A V Q S K L
B B E R M Y D Q R X F L A N
```

Atoll
Basin
Berm
Butte
Canyon
Cave
Creek
Delta
Desert
Divide
Fault
Forest
Glacier
Highland
Hill
Island
Isthmus
Lake
Mesa
Mountain
Ocean
Peninsula
Plateau
River
Seamount
Sound
Stream
Valley
Volcano

NIGHT THINGS WORD SEARCH

Bats
Bedtime
Blanket
Campfire
Cicadas
Dark
Darkness
Dinner
Dusk
Evening
Firefly
Halloween
Meteor
Midnight
Moon
Nocturnal
Owl
Pajamas
Planet
Sleep
Sleepover
Snoring
Stars
Storm
Story
Sunset
Toothbrush
Wolves
Yawn

```
S N N L L V L P L K P Y P T
K U Q A O T T Z A B S K L D
T E K N A L B E N O T U M T
H O I P O I L M R X X E D W
F V S T A R S G U K D K N M
P K L A R E S N T U E W Q I
T N Y Q D W E N C W A T D D
R X G X U A D U O Y G I O N
N K S W D M C A N R O R M I
I E C A M P F I R E I E M G
A H E R A P Y Y C K T N V H
I O Z W E W L R A E N D G T
F Y A E O F I G O W C E T H
D K L V E L L R P J Y H S Z
Z S B R J S L Y U K G D J S
S T I H V O B A R U N Q I Z
G F E K W E U E H L I Z U I
H H P S D X V R T E N A L P
F Y W T N O F K D B E S I E
S G I Q P U K A U H V E S D
S M W E N S S Q M J E V T H
E T E P A J A M A S V L O K
P L O T Y S N S J L I O R Z
S V S R B A O K R A D W Y P
O W L A M Z O H I Z I I E D
E E T R W R M O Y W N M D M
T S I G J N D R U L N X A E
H S U R B H T O O T E L Q V
D T P T Y N X D E E R G L O
```

ROAD TRIP WORD SEARCH

```
H W R C D E E P S X A D K H
I B L C O S A G T O U J I F
B E Z J R N E P O A C X D S
A S T V O F V S L J S I N N
Q E Y A S G H E L H R F R A
D C R E T Z D T R E H O U C
E Q M A U S Q O C T Y Y T K
K A R E T N Y T S U I Y U S
G G L Q H S I X Y X Q B S C
R R R E W O E B Z G U E L J
B T G H N A F R K O I V X E
G V Y S C O O L E R B Q L H
H O T E L Y T S I L Y A L P
P G Z M E R Z R P B L E C A
O I N L A B N C S A P M Z R
A E O V M H I K H I M V Z L
Q X E R U Q Y N D M G D L F
P L L Q K A I I E E O N R U
S I T A W V P R S N H T V H
S Q C H F F D D T O A Y E N
F J G N R M M S I I R R W L
Y I C O I H U R N T E Q E B
H R U V S C S Z A A I U C T
U T E P N C I B T C F D G F
E A K N W C C G I A P A R K
G B R Q I F H C O V D Z B B
X S Z C M D A U N L C X W Q
H Z W I U R I N J T H M G Z
C L E X P Q W W O R R A J V
```

Arrow
Car
Convertible
Cooler
Destination
Diner
Directions
Drink
Fuel
Games
Gas
Highway
Hotel
Map
Motel
Music
Park
Picnic
Playlist
Rest Area
Route
Sign
Snacks
Speed
State
Toll
Travel
U-Turn
Vacation

THINGS IN THE CITY WORD SEARCH

Airport
Apartment
Bakery
Bodega
Boulevard
Building
Car
Church
Deli
Diner
Dock
Factory
Ferry
Hospital
Library
Lights
Mosque
Museum
Pigeon
Police Station
Port
Restaurant
School
Skyscraper
Subway
Taxi
Temple
Train
Trolley

```
T T R D S A J S V I P J D Y
B E A S Z Y P P C Q O I A R
O G K X F B F A T R X L E O
U Q W R I H O D R T T E E T
L V J R A X A V N T Z D E C
E B M T G M U L K V M Q M A
V O W S K Y S C R A P E R F
A D A V Y Q E R B L P Z N T
R E K Z F C O U E B I D X T
D G D D V R I K Q M X Z Y S
W A N E S L Y Y H S R E D N
T Z D K D R W I C T O A J O
T K R I A R N S N K Q M F I
E I N R T M E A L O V A K T
M G B M A R R S C H O O L A
P I T I Q U O E T L I D U T
L O F L A T I P S O H Z L S
E N X T H I R L R D X D W E
F X S M Q U T H M I I M T C
B E T R O L L E Y N A U X I
R A B O O N Q S E R P E C L
D B K B O E W R U M L S H O
Y Z Y E X B B K C B K U M P
N M G Q R M H H F C W M E X
E I O I D Y U P O Y L A L A
P V A P W R L D P O R T Y B
V O E R C I O R C B H A T G
O H D H T S T H G I L T C L
K A L Y R R E F J Z O M T V
```

THINGS IN THE SKY WORD SEARCH

```
H W R C D E E P S X A D K H
I B L C O S A G T O U J I F
B E Z J R N E P O A C X D S
A S T V O F V S L J S I N N
Q E Y A S G H E L H R F R A
D C R E T Z D T R E H O U C
E Q M A U S Q O C T Y Y T K
K A R E T N Y T S U I Y U S
G G L Q H S I X Y X Q B S C
R R R E W O E B Z G U E L J
B T G H N A F R K O I V X E
G V Y S C O O L E R B Q L H
H O T E L Y T S I L Y A L P
P G Z M E R Z R P B L E C A
O I N L A B N C S A P M Z R
A E O V M H I K H I M V Z L
Q X E R U Q Y N D M G D L F
P L L Q K A I I E E O N R U
S I T A W V P R S N H T V H
S Q C H F F D D T O A Y E N
F J G N R M M S I I R R W L
Y I C O I H U R N T E Q E B
H R U V S C S Z A A I U C T
U T E P N C I B T C F D G F
E A K N W C C G I A P A R K
G B R Q I F H C O V D Z B B
X S Z C M D A U N L C X W Q
H Z W I U R I N J T H M G Z
C L E X P Q W W O R R A J V
```

Airplane
Aurora
Balloon
Bats
Big Dipper
Bird
Blimp
Cloud
Constellation
Eagle
Eclipse
Fireworks
Galaxy
Glider
Kite
Lightning
Mars
Meteor
Milky Way
Parachute
Planet
Rain
Rainbow
Satellite
Snow
Storm
Sun
Sunlight
Venus

Why are passengers in airplanes so polite to each other?

For fear of falling out!

When does an automobile go exactly as fast as a train?

When it's ON the train.

How to: Dot-to-Dots

Draw lines between the
numbers on the puzzle,
starting from 1 to 2, and then
continuing, until the picture
puzzle is complete.

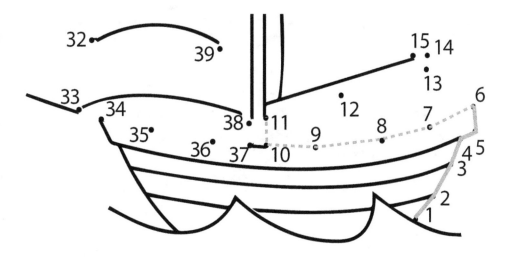

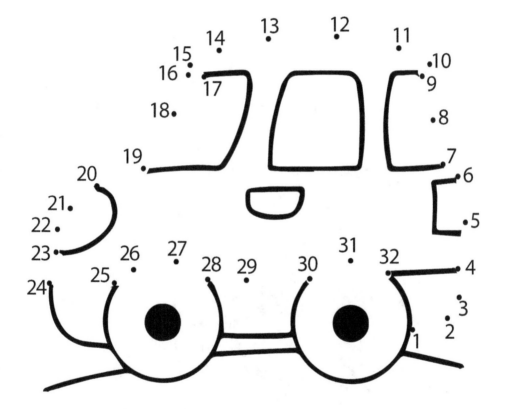

13
12
14
11
15
•10
16
9
17
8
18
7
19
6
20
5
21
22
23
26 27 31 32
25 28 29 30 4
24 3
2
1

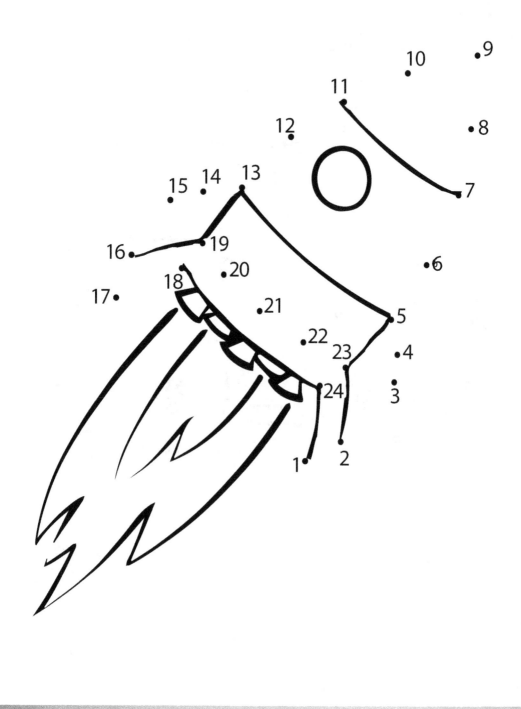

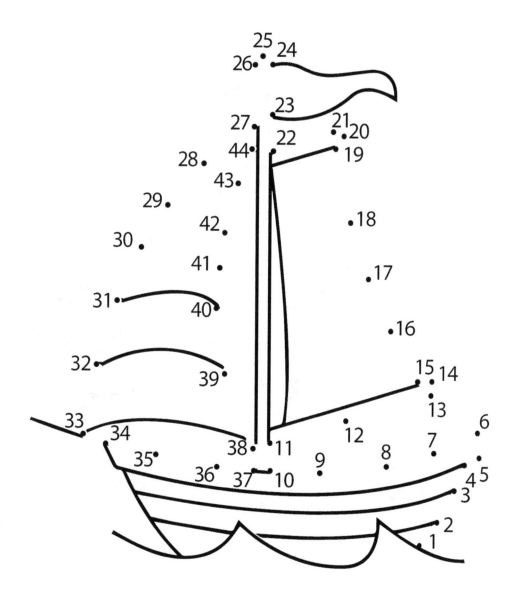

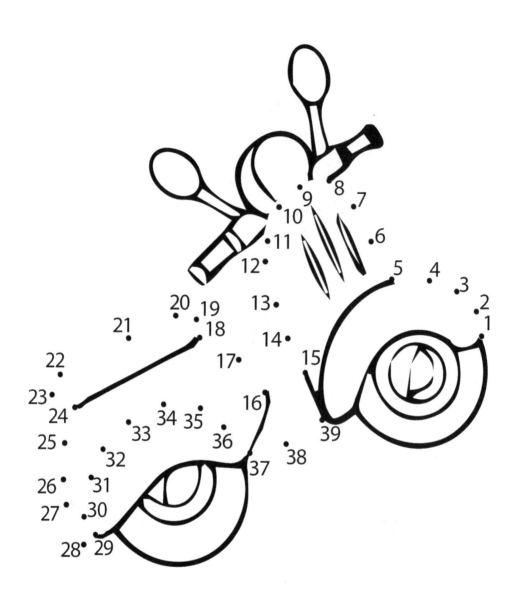

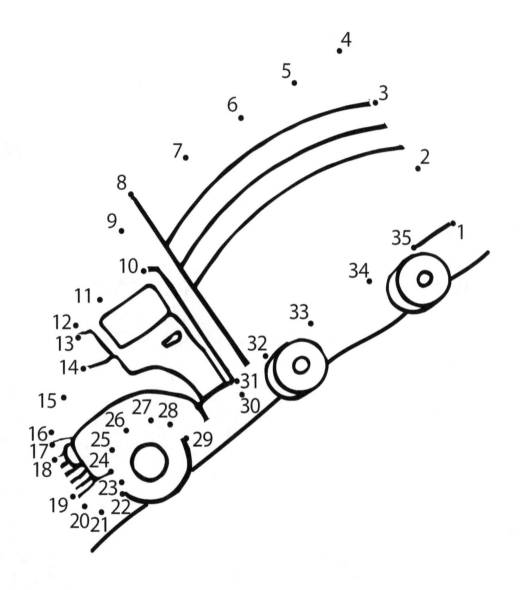

Why is the emblem of the United States more enduring than that of France, England, Ireland or Scotland?

The "lily" may fade and its leaves decay,
The "rose" from its stem may sever,
The "shamrock" and "thistle" may pass away,
But the "stars" will shine forever.

If you threw a white stone into the Red Sea, what would it become?

A WET stone!

How to:
Find-the-Difference

Can you spot all the
differences?

Circle all the differences
between the two pictures.
Each puzzle has between 6, 8,
or 10 differences, and you can
find answer keys at the back
of the book.

Good luck!

FiND 6 DiFFERENCES

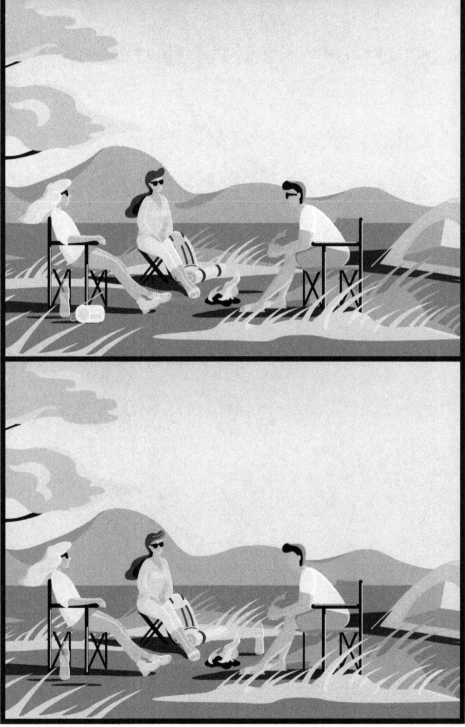

What kind of ears does an engine possess?

Engineers.

Why are the western prairies so flat?

Because the sun sets on them every night.

How to: Cryptograms

This is a decoding puzzle. Decipher the quoted phrase by finding the substitute letters. Each puzzle will have a hint! Sometimes it's about the person who said it, and others are about the quote itself.

Careful—sometimes the missing letter and its code letter could be the same.

Here's a hint...

What handheld object can help you go on an imaginary journey?

A	B	C	D	E	F	G	H	I	J	K	L	M
P	Q		L				Y				N	
N	O	P	Q	R	S	T	U	V	W	X	Y	Z
							X					

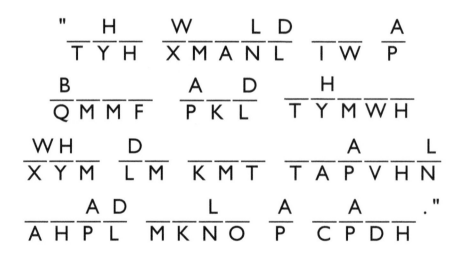

" _H_ _W_ _L_D _ _ _A
  T Y H   X M A N L   I W   P

_B_ _ _ _A_ D _H_ _
Q M M F   P K L   T Y M W H

WH_ _D _ _ _ _A_ _L
X Y M   L M   K M T   T A P V H N

_ _ _A D _ _L _A_ _A_ ."
A H P L   M K N O   P   C P D H

- SAINT AUGUSTINE

Here's a hint...

What word starts with a "D" that can mean
bold and adventurous?

A	B	C	D	E	F	G	H	I	J	K	L	M
			I			F		V			G	
N	O	P	Q	R	S	T	U	V	W	X	Y	Z
					P							

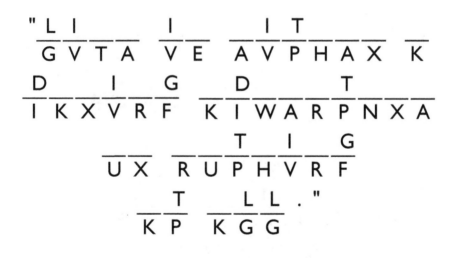

" L I ___ I ___ ___ I T ___ ___ ___ ___
  G V T A V E A V P H A X K

D ___ I ___ G ___ D ___ ___ ___ T ___ ___ ___
I K X V R F K I W A R P N X A

___ ___ ___ ___ ___ T ___ I ___ G
U X R U P H V R F

___ ___ T ___ L L . "
K P K G G

- HELEN KELLER

Here's a hint...

What country is also the name of a continent?

A	B	C	D	E	F	G	H	I	J	K	L	M
D												

N	O	P	Q	R	S	T	U	V	W	X	Y	Z
R			P						H		T	

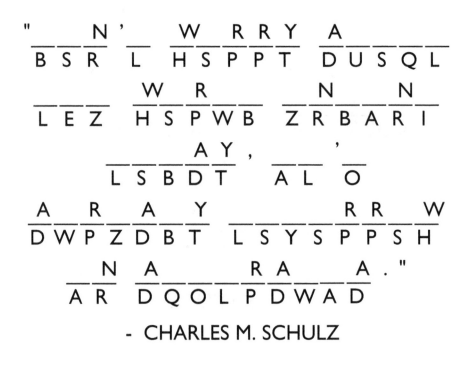

```
"  __ N ' __  W __ R R Y __ A __
   B S R   L  H S P P T   D U S Q L

   __ __ __   W __ R __ __   N __ __ N __
   L  E  Z   H S P W B   Z R B A R I

          __ __ A Y ,   __ __ ' __
          L S B D T   A L   O

   A __ R __ A __ Y __ __ __ R R __ W
   D W P Z D B T   L S Y S P P S H

      __ N __ A __ __ __ R A __ __ A . "
      A R   D Q O L P D W A D
```

- CHARLES M. SCHULZ

Here's a hint...

This is something to look forward to.

A	B	C	D	E	F	G	H	I	J	K	L	M
T			F					N				

N	O	P	Q	R	S	T	U	V	W	X	Y	Z
V		B			E			X			G	

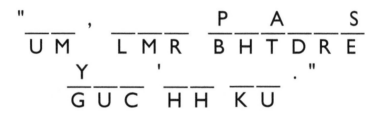

```
"  __ ,  ___   _P_A__S
   U M    L M R   B H T D R E
      __ ' __  __ . "
      G U C  H H  K U
```

- DR. SEUSS

Here's a hint...

This quote mentions a chocolatey dessert treat.

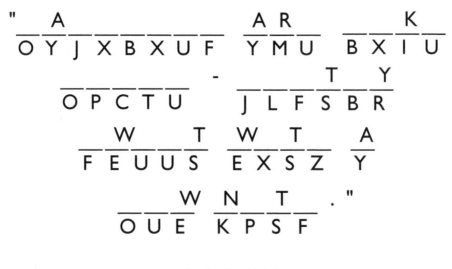

A	B	C	D	E	F	G	H	I	J	K	L	M
Y										I		
N	O	P	Q	R	S	T	U	V	W	X	Y	Z
K			M		S				E		R	

```
"    A                    A R         K
 O Y J X B X U F      Y M U      B X I U

                -              T     Y
     O P C T U          J L F S B R

        W       T    W    T      A
     F E U U S      E X S Z    Y

           W    N    T    . "
        O U E    K P S F
```

- LES DAWSON

Here's a hint...

What place do you arrive at when you're done traveling?

A	B	C	D	E	F	G	H	I	J	K	L	M
A					K					H		

N	O	P	Q	R	S	T	U	V	W	X	Y	Z
				N		P		Y				

```
"  _  F  _      _  S      A
   J  I  K  Z   I  N      A

   _  _  U  _  _  Y  ,    _  _  _
   C  S  P  F  W  Z  O    W  S  U

   A   _  S  _     _  A  _  _  _  .  "
   A   Q  Z  N  U  I  W  A  U  I  S  W
```

- RALPH WALDO EMERSON

Why isn't distance at sea measured by miles as it is on land?

Because it is "knot".

Which road goes from New York to Chicago without once moving an inch?

The RAILroad tracks.

HOW to:
WOUld You Rather?

Share these questions aloud with your family & friends for extra fun.

You can explain your answers and be creative with the reasons why!

What would YOU rather do? Is it the same as what your family & friends prefer?

would you rather...

Take a week-long vacation touring a foreign country or take a week-long vacation touring the country you live in?

would you rather...

Be stranded on a deserted island with only coconuts to eat or be stranded on a deserted island with only coffee to drink?

would you rather...

Take a trip to the moon or take a trip to Mars?

would you rather...

Visit the Magic Kingdom at Disneyland or visit the Wizarding World of Harry Potter at Universal Studios?

WOULD you rather...

Ride an elephant on an African safari or ride a camel around the Egyptian pyramids?

WOULD you rather...

Travel across the country in a private Learjet or travel across the country in the Batmobile?

WOULD you rather...

Climb Mount Everest in Asia (the tallest mountain in the world) or spelunk through the Krubera cave in Cagra, Georgia (the deepest cave on earth)?

WOULD you rather...

Eat only fruits and vegetables on your vacation or eat only pizza and tacos on your vacation?

would you rather...

Pitch a tent near a lake with kayaks and s'mores or stay in a fancy hotel with a water park and room service?

would you rather...

Spend your vacation on a beach, boating and surfing or spend your vacation in the mountains, skiing and horseback riding?

would you rather...

Eat live octopus in Japan or eat escargot (snails) in France?

would you rather...

Hang out with a panda bear in China or hang out with a gorilla in Africa?

would you rather...
Go to the North Pole for Christmas or go to Disney World for spring break?

would you rather...
Be stuck in a motel room infested with lizards or be stuck on a bus infested with spiders?

would you rather...
Swim in the hotel pool or relax in the room with pizza and a movie after a long day of travel?

would you rather...
Meet a cowboy in Montana or meet an astronaut in Texas?

Would you rather...
Stay in a castle while on vacation or stay in a beach house while on vacation?

Would you rather...
Go deep-sea diving in the ocean or go skydiving from an airplane?

Would you rather...
Take a million dollars on your trip that you can't spend on yourself or take a million dollars on your trip that you can't share with anyone?

Would you rather...
Have the superpower of teleportation on your travels or have the superpower of invisibility on your travels?

would you rather...

Only be able to wear pants and a sweatshirt on your travels or only be able to wear your swimsuit on your travels?

would you rather...

Discover a hidden treasure on a sunken ship or discover an alien on a UFO?

would you rather...

Travel across the country in the car listening to the same song over and over or travel across the country in the car in silence?

would you rather...

Take a magic wizard on your trip with you or take a superhero on your trip with you?

What was the largest island before Australia was discovered?

Australia was always the largest.

What is the difference between the North Pole and the South Pole?

All the Difference in the world.

How to:
Dots and Boxes

This game is played with two players! Each player takes turns to join two adjacent dots with a horizontal OR vertical line (no diagonals).

If you complete the fourth side of a box on your turn, you must draw another line.

Mark your boxes with a unique letter, so you can count to see who won.

What is the largest rope in the world?

Europe!

Which travels faster, heat or cold?

Heat. You can catch a cold.

How to: Sudoku

Fill in the missing numbers to complete the puzzle. Every column, row, and grid must contain the numbers 1 through 9 without ANY repetition.

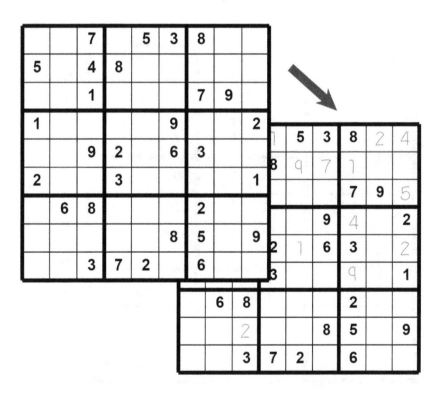

Puzzle 1

	2			7	1			9
4			5	3	2			1
			9				5	
9	1	5						
	7						9	
						1	7	6
	9				8			
6			7	1	4			8
7			6	2			4	

Done
1 ☐
2 ☐
3 ☐
4 ☐
5 ☐
6 ☐
7 ☐
8 ☐
9 ☐

Puzzle 2

9	2	4			7	8		
				6	9		4	
8					3	7		
			9			6		7
3								1
7		6			1			
		7	6					5
	9		1	4				
		8	7			1	2	4

Done
1 ☐
2 ☐
3 ☐
4 ☐
5 ☐
6 ☐
7 ☐
8 ☐
9 ☐

Puzzle 1

5	2	4				7		
3	7						4	
6			3		4	1		
			1	4			3	
	4			2			6	
	6			3	9			
		8	6		2			7
	1						2	9
		5				6	8	4

Done

1 ☐
2 ☐
3 ☐
4 ☐
5 ☐
6 ☐
7 ☐
8 ☐
9 ☐

Puzzle 2

	3			7			1	
6			1					
1						4	8	
9					1	6		8
	6	1	7	4	8	3	5	
4		3	5					2
	5	2						4
				2				5
	4			9		3		

Done

1 ☐
2 ☐
3 ☐
4 ☐
5 ☐
6 ☐
7 ☐
8 ☐
9 ☐

Done
1 ☐ 2 ☐ 3 ☐ 4 ☐ 5 ☐ 6 ☐ 7 ☐ 8 ☐ 9 ☐

Puzzle 1:

					1			
9					3	7		
	5	6		2			3	
7		5	8			3		
6	8	2				9	7	5
		3			7	8		2
	4			3		1	6	
		1	9					3
			1					

Done
1 ☐ 2 ☐ 3 ☐ 4 ☐ 5 ☐ 6 ☐ 7 ☐ 8 ☐ 9 ☐

Puzzle 2:

			5		3	4		
	5		9				3	
3		6				1		5
4	8					5		
1		9		4		3		2
		5					7	4
9		2				8		1
	6				8		4	
		7	1		9			

Puzzle 1

7	9			4				
1					7	8		
	8		9				3	
	7	6	2					8
	5	9				2	7	
2					3	4	5	
	6				5		9	
		7	1					2
				8			6	5

Done
1 ☐
2 ☐
3 ☐
4 ☐
5 ☐
6 ☐
7 ☐
8 ☐
9 ☐

Puzzle 2

1								3
	4				7	1	9	8
	3		6			5		
	9		4	7		2		
8								7
		5		6	3		4	
		9			8		3	
5	8	3	7				1	
7								6

Done
1 ☐
2 ☐
3 ☐
4 ☐
5 ☐
6 ☐
7 ☐
8 ☐
9 ☐

Done
1 ☐
2 ☐
3 ☐
4 ☐
5 ☐
6 ☐
7 ☐
8 ☐
9 ☐

Done
1 ☐
2 ☐
3 ☐
4 ☐
5 ☐
6 ☐
7 ☐
8 ☐
9 ☐

Puzzle 1

	7		8			1	9	
		5						
8		3	1				5	2
				3			6	9
		8	2		5	3		
3	5			1				
9	3				2	6		1
						9		
	4	1			3		2	

Done

1 ☐ 2 ☐ 3 ☐ 4 ☐ 5 ☐ 6 ☐ 7 ☐ 8 ☐ 9 ☐

Puzzle 2

	8			3	7		2	
5	2	1			8		3	
7								
8				7	4	2		
		5		6		4		
		2	1	5				8
								2
	5		4			3	6	9
	6		5	2			1	

Done

1 ☐ 2 ☐ 3 ☐ 4 ☐ 5 ☐ 6 ☐ 7 ☐ 8 ☐ 9 ☐

What state is round at both ends and high in the middle?

Ohio!

Why should you never complain about the price of a railroad ticket?

Because it is "fair" (fare).

How to: Hidden Pictures

Explore a different location
from 6 different continents.

Find all of the hidden images,
listed in the box at the bottom
of the page, inside the larger
picture. You can circle them
on the picture itself, and cross
them off in the box below
once you've found them.

Good luck!

Explore...
The Sydney Opera House

Explore...
The Great Mayan Pyramid of Chichen Itza

Explore...
The Arc de Triomphe and Eiffel Tower

Explore...
The Statue of Liberty

Explore...
A Chinese New Year Festival

Explore...
The Great Sphinx & The Pyramids of Egypt

Why was the wheel the greatest thing ever invented?

Because it got things rolling.

What ten-letter word starts with gas?

Automobile.

How to:
ReBus Puzzles

These puzzles are word-based brain teasers that describe a word or phrase without spelling it out. Sometimes there are clues in the positioning of words and letters. Other times, you'll have to add, subtract, or replace letters to form a new word or phrase. They can be tricky, so think creatively!

Deciphering the clues is what makes rebuses such fun!

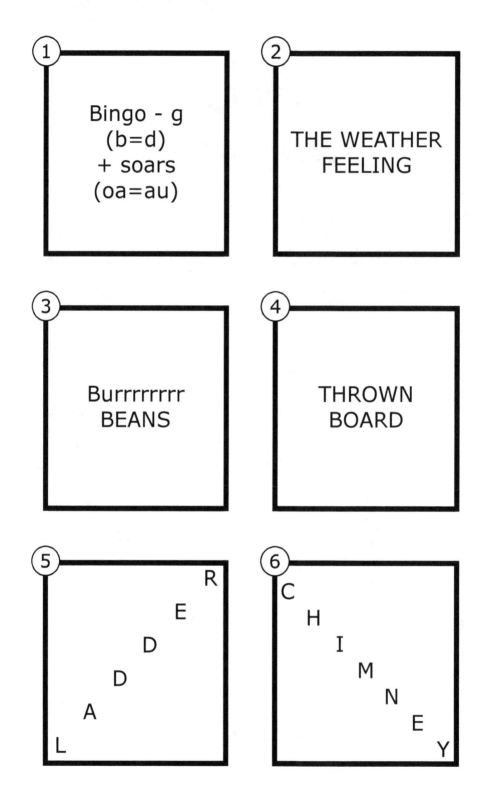

1

Bingo - g
(b=d)
+ soars
(oa=au)

2

THE WEATHER
FEELING

3

Burrrrrrrr
BEANS

4

THROWN
BOARD

5

R
E
D
D
A
L

6

C
H
I
M
N
E
Y

7

Jack-in-the-box
- in-the-box
+ o
+ banter (b=l)
+ n

8

O L L

R   E

                    R

9

THE BRIDGE
WATER

10

THEallFAMILY

11

A

          T

N   O

     W

12

The Dwarf
    Dwarf
        Dwarf
            Dwarf
                Dwarf
                    Dwarf
                        Dwarf

13. Red biding (b=r) mood (m=h)

14. Mice, Dress, Shoe, Stepsisters

15. Ocean, Lobster, Villain, Singing

16. Z Z Z Beauty

17. 4 + lead (d=f) + c + rover (r=l)

18. Addition, Subtraction, Division, Multiplication, Paper, Home

19

SPlostACE

20

Cast
- C
+ ro
+ net (e=au)

21

Sock
- k + c
+ her - h
+ fall (f=b)

22

The 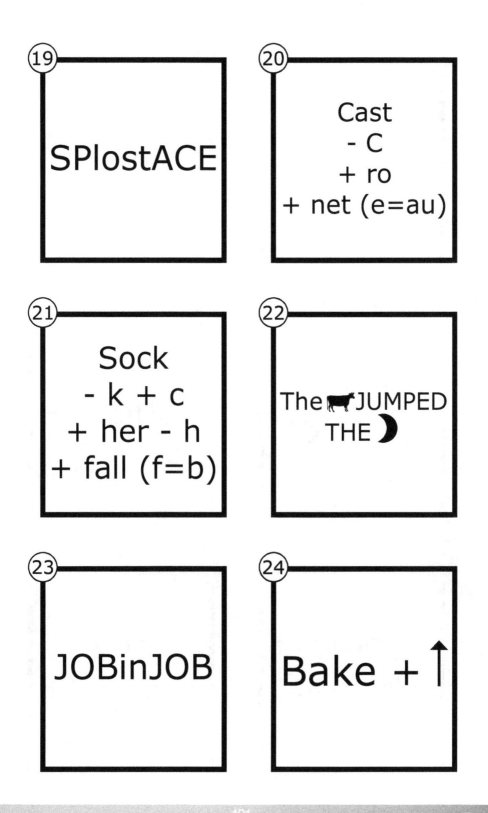JUMPED
THE 🌙

23

JOBinJOB

24

Bake + ↑

25 TRAFstuckFIC

26 CAdrivingRS

27 GAME
, SORRY

28 MOUfootTH

29 STAND?
DO YOU

30 JUMP
THE FENCE

31

Blender
(ble=thu)
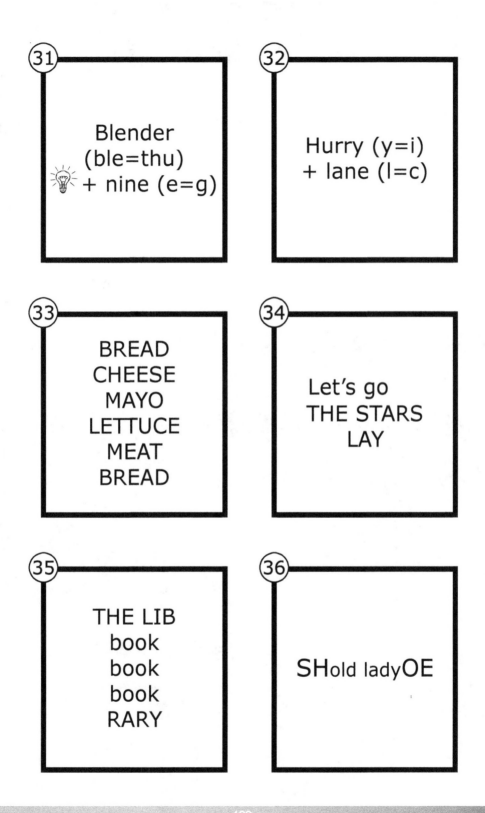 + nine (e=g)

32

Hurry (y=i)
+ lane (l=c)

33

BREAD
CHEESE
MAYO
LETTUCE
MEAT
BREAD

34

Let's go
THE STARS
LAY

35

THE LIB
book
book
book
RARY

36

SHold ladyOE

What can speak all the languages of the world?

An echo!

What falls and doesn't break?

Night falls (Day Breaks).

How to:
Step-By-Step Drawing

Using a pencil, follow each drawing diagram step by step. Don't worry about being perfect—just keep practicing! Once you've finished your pencil drawing, you can trace it with a black pen and color it to your liking.

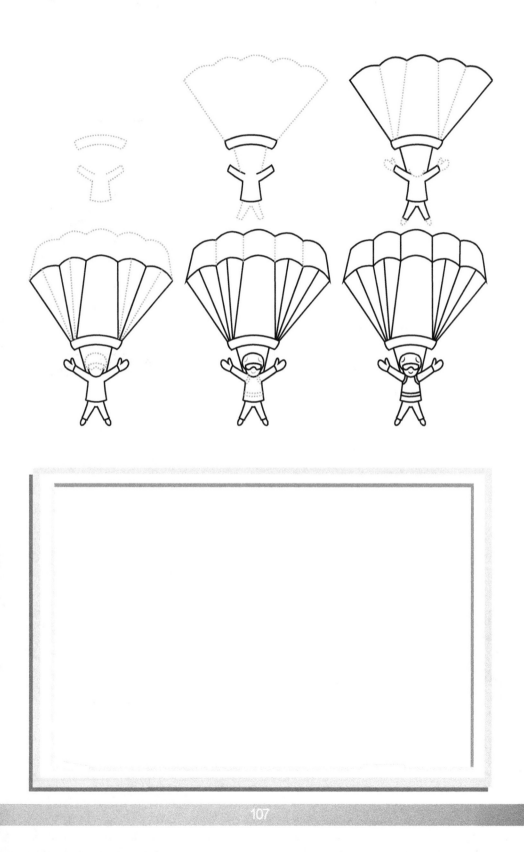

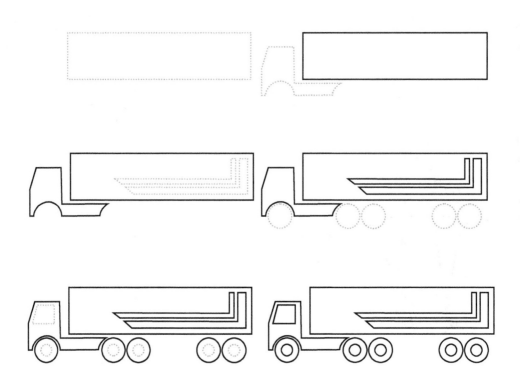

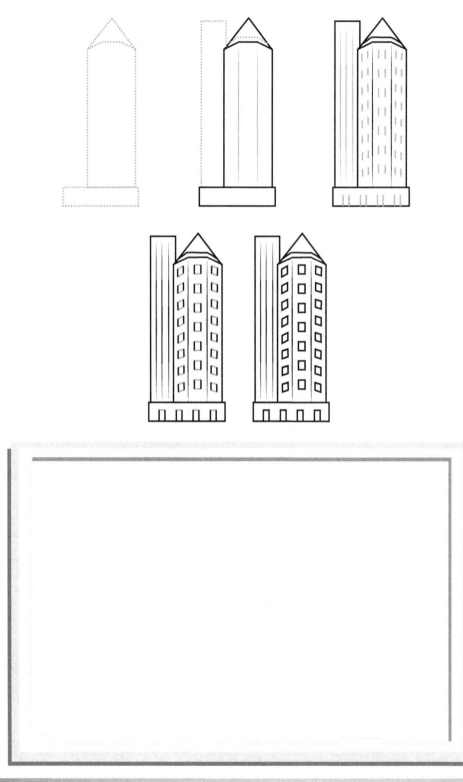

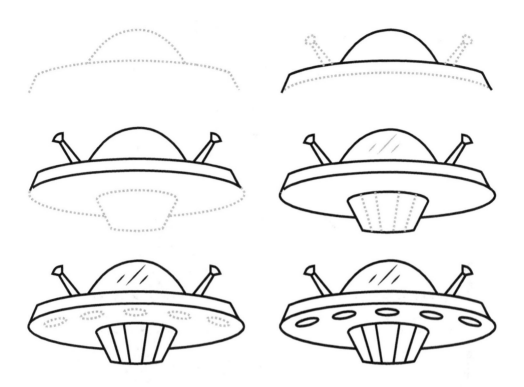

ANSWER KEYS
FIND-THE-DIFFERENCE

ANSWER KEYS
CRYPTOGRAMS

"THE WORLD IS A BOOK AND THOSE WHO DO NOT TRAVEL READ ONLY A PAGE."

"LIFE IS EITHER A DARING ADVENTURE OR NOTHING AT ALL."

"DON'T WORRY ABOUT THE WORLD ENDING TODAY, IT'S ALREADY TOMORROW IN AUSTRALIA."

"OH, THE PLACES YOU'LL GO."

"FAMILIES ARE LIKE FUDGE - MOSTLY SWEET WITH A FEW NUTS."

"LIFE IS A JOURNEY, NOT A DESTINATION."

ANSWER KEYS
SUDOKU

5	2	8	4	7	1	3	6	9
4	6	9	5	3	2	7	8	1
1	3	7	9	8	6	4	5	2
9	1	5	2	6	7	8	3	4
8	7	6	1	4	3	2	9	5
3	4	2	8	9	5	1	7	6
2	9	4	3	5	8	6	1	7
6	5	3	7	1	4	9	2	8
7	8	1	6	2	9	5	4	3

5	2	4	8	6	1	7	9	3
3	7	1	2	9	5	8	4	6
6	8	9	3	7	4	1	5	2
9	5	7	1	4	6	2	3	8
1	4	3	7	2	8	9	6	5
8	6	2	5	3	9	4	7	1
4	9	8	6	5	2	3	1	7
7	1	6	4	8	3	5	2	9
2	3	5	9	1	7	6	8	4

9	2	4	5	1	7	8	6	3
1	7	3	8	6	9	5	4	2
8	6	5	4	2	3	7	1	9
2	5	1	9	8	4	6	3	7
3	8	9	2	7	6	4	5	1
7	4	6	3	5	1	2	9	8
4	1	7	6	3	2	9	8	5
5	9	2	1	4	8	3	7	6
6	3	8	7	9	5	1	2	4

5	3	8	2	7	4	9	1	6
6	9	4	1	8	3	5	2	7
1	2	7	9	5	6	4	8	3
9	7	5	3	2	1	6	4	8
2	6	1	7	4	8	3	5	9
4	8	3	5	6	9	1	7	2
3	5	2	6	1	7	8	9	4
8	1	9	4	3	2	7	6	5
7	4	6	8	9	5	2	3	1

8	3	7	4	5	1	6	2	9
9	2	4	6	8	3	7	5	1
1	5	6	7	2	9	4	3	8
7	1	5	8	9	2	3	4	6
6	8	2	3	1	4	9	7	5
4	9	3	5	6	7	8	1	2
5	4	9	2	3	8	1	6	7
2	7	1	9	4	6	5	8	3
3	6	8	1	7	5	2	9	4

7	9	3	5	4	8	6	2	1
1	2	5	6	3	7	8	4	9
6	8	4	9	2	1	5	3	7
3	7	6	2	5	4	9	1	8
4	5	9	8	1	6	2	7	3
2	1	8	7	9	3	4	5	6
8	6	2	3	7	5	1	9	4
5	4	7	1	6	9	3	8	2
9	3	1	4	8	2	7	6	5

ANSWER KEYS
SUDOKU

Grid 1

2	1	8	5	6	3	4	9	7
7	5	4	9	1	2	6	3	8
3	9	6	7	8	4	1	2	5
4	8	3	2	9	7	5	1	6
1	7	9	6	4	5	3	8	2
6	2	5	8	3	1	9	7	4
9	3	2	4	7	6	8	5	1
5	6	1	3	2	8	7	4	9
8	4	7	1	5	9	2	6	3

Grid 2

1	5	7	9	8	4	6	2	3
6	4	2	5	3	7	1	9	8
9	3	8	6	1	2	5	7	4
3	9	6	4	7	1	2	8	5
8	1	4	2	9	5	3	6	7
2	7	5	8	6	3	9	4	1
4	6	9	1	5	8	7	3	2
5	8	3	7	2	6	4	1	9
7	2	1	3	4	9	8	5	6

Grid 3

9	7	5	2	3	1	6	4	8
4	1	3	9	6	8	7	5	2
2	8	6	7	5	4	9	3	1
7	5	1	6	8	2	4	9	3
8	4	9	3	1	5	2	7	6
6	3	2	4	7	9	1	8	5
5	2	7	8	9	6	3	1	4
1	9	4	5	2	3	8	6	7
3	6	8	1	4	7	5	2	9

Grid 4

2	7	6	8	5	4	1	9	3
4	1	5	3	2	9	7	8	6
8	9	3	1	6	7	4	5	2
1	2	4	7	3	8	5	6	9
7	6	8	2	9	5	3	1	4
3	5	9	4	1	6	2	7	8
9	3	7	5	8	2	6	4	1
5	8	2	6	4	1	9	3	7
6	4	1	9	7	3	8	2	5

Grid 5

9	2	8	1	4	3	5	7	6
3	6	1	5	9	7	4	8	2
5	4	7	8	6	2	9	3	1
4	7	9	3	2	8	1	6	5
1	3	5	9	7	6	2	4	8
2	8	6	4	1	5	3	9	7
7	5	4	2	8	9	6	1	3
6	9	2	7	3	1	8	5	4
8	1	3	6	5	4	7	2	9

Grid 6

6	8	4	9	3	7	1	2	5
5	2	1	6	4	8	9	3	7
7	3	9	2	1	5	8	4	6
8	9	6	3	7	4	2	5	1
1	7	5	8	6	2	4	9	3
3	4	2	1	5	9	6	7	8
4	1	3	7	9	6	5	8	2
2	5	7	4	8	1	3	6	9
9	6	8	5	2	3	7	1	4

ANSWER KEYS
HIDDEN PICTURES

Explore...
The Sydney Opera House

Explore...
The Great Mayan Pyramid of Chichen Itza

Explore...
The Arc de Triomphe and Eiffel Tower

ANSWER KEYS
HIDDEN PICTURES

Explore...
The Statue of Liberty

Explore...
A Chinese New Year Festival

Explore...
The Great Sphinx & The Pyramids of Egypt

ANSWER KEYS
REBUS PUZZLES

1. Dinosaurs
2. Feeling under the weather
3. Cool beans
4. Thrown overboard
5. Climbing ladders
6. Climbing down the chimney
7. Jack-o-lantern
8. Roller coaster
9. Water under the bridge
10. All in the family
11. Around town
12. The seven dwarfs
13. Little red riding hood
14. Cinderella
15. Little Mermaid
16. Sleeping Beauty
17. Four leaf clover
18. Math homework
19. Lost in space
20. Astronaut
21. Soccer ball
22. The cow jumped over the moon
23. In between jobs
24. Make-up
25. Stuck in traffic
26. Driving in cars
27. Game over, sorry
28. Foot in mouth
29. Do you understand?
30. Jump over the fence
31. Thunder & lightning
32. Hurricane
33. Sandwich
34. Let's go lay under the stars
35. Books in the library
36. The little old lady who lived in the shoe